Pixie,
the Philosopher's Cat

Pixie,
the Philosopher's Cat

Maria daVenza Tillmanns

IGUANA

Copyright © 2025 Maria daVenza Tillmanns
Published by Iguana Books
720 Bathurst Street
Toronto, ON M5S 2R4

All rights reserved. No part of this publication may be reproduced, stored in a retrieval system or transmitted, in any form or by any means, electronic, mechanical, recording or otherwise (except brief passages for purposes of review) without the prior permission of the author.

Rachel's cat Pixie was the inspiration for this story, when Maria cat-sat her and took these photos.
Photos of Pixie the cat: Maria daVenza Tillmanns

All paintings by C.H. daVenza Tillmanns, b. Carrara, Italy, 1893, d. Bad Godesberg, Germany, 1964. Where information is available, titles and dates have been provided.
Photos of C.H. daVenza Tillmanns's paintings: GertJan Keizer, The Netherlands

Publisher: Cheryl Hawley
Editor: Holly Warren

ISBN 978-1-77180-737-1 (paperback)
ISBN 978-1-77180-738-8 (hardcover)
ISBN 978-1-77180-736-4 (epub)

This is an original print edition of *Pixie, the Philosopher's Cat*.

Dedicated to Pixie Cat

Before she realized what was happening, the Philosopher saw Pixie leap through the air and land on top of the bookcase, which overflowed with all sorts of books — ones on philosophy, of course, but also some on mythology and psychology and quite a few filled with fairy tales from around the world.

She sat in her favorite chair and sipped her freshly brewed tea while she watched her calico diligently wash her face on her new perch. Seeing Pixie on top of her bookcase, the Philosopher was reminded how she enjoyed engaging Pixie in the questions she contemplated as she read, often asking her, What do you think? What would you do? Pixie, who lived in a world so different from hers, opened a new stream of thinking for the Philosopher, who liked to entertain ideas from various perspectives and explore unique ways of seeing the world.

Pixie and the Philosopher shared the same inquisitive and curious spirit and both looked upon the world as a place full of discoveries to be made. Rather than it being something to just *know* about, the world to them was something to *wonder* and *ponder* about. Pixie and the Philosopher were always trying to figure things out, because nothing ever seemed to be quite the same.

As she watched Pixie and glanced down at the bookcase, the Philosopher's attention was drawn to a little book she so much loved — *The Real Thief*, written and illustrated by William Steig. The Philosopher loved Steig's illustrations. He had also been a cartoonist for *The New Yorker* magazine, she remembered. She decided to take the book down from the shelf and read it once again.

The Philosopher always felt that reading a book again provided new perspectives. You never quite read a book the same way, she thought. It changes over time. Always. It's as though books live a life of their own, much like everything in her apartment — it was a living space, after all, and the Philosopher loved to surround herself with life. For instance, she kept many plants in every room. Plants, too, had a life of their own, she thought as she looked around. And so do paintings, she realized. She stood up and took in the art around her, appreciating the several paintings she had painted herself — which, she had to admit, she quite liked — and admiring the ones done by her grandfather. These she absolutely loved.

Although the Philosopher had never known her grandfather, she felt close to him through his artwork and loved the story that had been passed down to her about his adventurous life. He had lived in Europe and Indonesia and he was a great inventor as well as an artist. A Renaissance man! she thought. Sadly, although he'd been well respected in his time, World War II ruined his career as an artist. He'd been working in Paris when the war broke out and had been forced to leave. She had been told that he'd taken classes with André Lhote, and counted famous artists Georges Braque, Alberto Giacometti and Piet Mondrian among his friends.

The Philosopher had kept a beautiful review of her grandfather's work that had been written by the then well-respected art critic Marcel Sauvage. The Philosopher had always thought the world needed to see her grandfather's great work. Although two of his paintings had already been donated to a museum in Holland, the Philosopher was always trying to think of ways to get more of his art into the world.

She also felt that where he had left off, she would continue; he was a painter and she, a free-thinker and philosopher. His pieces had a penetrating quality that revealed a contemplative way of seeing the world in much the same way philosophy does. She and her grandfather both seemed to share a deep understanding of the world as well as a connection through their work and across time.

She approached the bookcase and stretched out her hand to give Pixie a scratch under her chin — the bookcase was quite high.

Marble Quarry in Carrara, 1941

"...as she looked at her sweet 16-year-old cat's adorable, mottled face."

The Philosopher looked at Pixie, amazed at how rich her life had been as a result of sharing her home with this creature. She smiled as she looked at her sweet 16-year-old cat's adorable, mottled face. The Philosopher mused and smiled, thinking about how her small apartment contained so much life. Everything in it was so full of life — books, plants, paintings and her darling cat. She breathed it all in.

Then she considered, Why do so many people yearn for purpose or meaning in their lives, when — it seemed to her, at least — life itself was inherently meaningful? And truly, would Pixie yearn to be something other than the cat she was? The Philosopher gently stroked Pixie's back and considered. No, she thought, Pixie wouldn't want to be anything other than Pixie.

The Philosopher felt a close bond with her cat. She felt she could communicate with her as she could with her books, plants and paintings. Communication didn't really depend that much on the use of words, she thought. It could take on many forms.

With book in hand, she returned to her favorite armchair and finished her tea. She then turned her attention to *The Real Thief*. The thing about books, she figured, is that they offer new insights every time you read them. There was always something new to discover. But, she wondered, is it possible to gain new insights if the inspiration for them isn't somehow in the book already? And if you get something new out of it each time you read it, were you reading the same book or a different book each time? And what about if someone else reads it? Are they reading the same book as you?

The Philosopher thought about these types of questions all the time. That's what made her a philosopher to begin with, of course.

She looked at the cover, then flipped through the book, pausing on each illustration. She loved Steig's visual interpretation of the story. The drawings were so expressive of the deep feelings the characters experienced — their pride, their joy, their pain, their sorrow.

She decided to move to her couch by the window where she could look out onto the trees that lined her street. Pixie jumped off the bookcase and followed the Philosopher to the couch. After the Philosopher was settled, Pixie curled up in her lap and purred quietly. The Philosopher flipped to the first page and dived into the familiar story about a goose named Gawain.

The story starts by explaining that Gawain was an honorable goose, trustworthy and upright. King Basil had chosen him to be the Chief Guard of his Royal Treasury and Gawain loved the King, as so many others in King Basil's kingdom did. He could not, would not, refuse the offer to be Chief Guard. It was a great honor.

Then the Philosopher paused and wondered aloud, How do we know when we can be sure someone — or some goose, in this case — can be trusted to be upright and honest?

Pixie, nestling on the Philosopher's lap, licked her hand and looked up. Could you somehow *feel* whether someone was truly trustworthy? the Philosopher considered. How did Pixie decide? What do we humans look for when we decide someone is a someone of integrity? Are we able to just feel it as well?

Maybe it is a feeling, she thought, but it's only over time that we can know. We never have any *real* proof ever, do we? And this idea, she realized, is at the heart of this delightful but also sad story.

So here is where the story takes on a real serious issue — the Philosopher continued looking at her cat — because in the story, the deeply trusted Gawain was suddenly no longer trusted. In fact, Gawain became the prime suspect of a serious crime.

Pixie licked her paw and again looked at the Philosopher. Well, of course you're confused, said the Philosopher. And rightly so! How can you not trust someone you previously trusted?

If you stopped trusting them, she pondered, did that necessarily mean *they* did something untrustworthy that broke your trust in them or that you never really trusted them to begin with regardless of what they did or didn't do? History is full of examples where

Le petit laboratoire de femme, 1960

Dream, 1955

people are not trusted for no reason. Women were not trusted to vote or work outside the house, for instance. And how silly is that! she mused. Could women even be trusted to be philosophers? She laughed at how absurd the world could be.

We often assume someone we trusted did something to lose our trust. But couldn't it also be true that the sudden loss of trust had to do with us and not at all with the person in question?

Why was Gawain, she thought, a goose of the highest integrity, suddenly doubted and now even a suspect of an unspeakable crime?

Where did the trust everyone had in Gawain go? Doesn't trust deserve to be respected? Why was Gawain not even given the benefit of the doubt by all who said they trusted him?

The Philosopher looked at her incredulous cat. Not just humans and cats — we all need trust relationships to survive, but our conception of trust may differ quite substantially. Or did it really? Trust is so basic to life.

One day, the story continues, Gawain noticed that some rubies were missing from the treasury. He counted again and again, but nothing changed the fact that the rubies simply weren't all there.

Gawain hurried to tell King Basil of this unfortunate discovery.

Both King Basil and Gawain — the Chief Guard, remember — went to the Royal Treasury only to realize that a total of 29 rubies were missing. How could that be?

King Basil was perturbed and looked at Gawain. How could anyone get in here, he asked, if only you and I have the keys?

It didn't take long for everyone in town to hear about the theft from the Royal Treasury. The townspeople were alarmed. King Basil was beside himself.

In the days that followed, even more tension built up in town when it was discovered that many gold pieces and silver ornaments

The Judge, 1955

were missing as well. And after that, even the world-famous Kalikak diamond went missing. The Philosopher did not know why the Kalikak diamond was world famous, and by the sounds of it, it must have been the only such diamond in the entire kingdom.

There was no accounting for their disappearance. And with the disappearance of the rubies, the gold pieces, the silver ornaments *and* the Kalikak diamond, the trust the King had in Gawain began to wane. The King started to doubt Gawain's honest declarations that he had nothing to do with the robberies and had no idea how they might have happened.

Pixie looked at the Philosopher with eyes half closed as though to say that trust in much of the human world was truly a fragile thing. I know, said the Philosopher emphatically. Instead of being something you could build on, trust between humans could so easily break under pressure.

But why? thought the Philosopher. She wasn't sure what the answer was. She would have to give it more thought, as always.

She decided to read on for a clue, remembering that Prime Minister Adrian played a pivotal role in how the deep trust between King Basil and Gawain had eroded.

Using flawless reasoning, Adrian argued that, since only he, the King and Gawain had the keys to the Royal Treasury and that surely the King could take from the Royal Treasury as he pleased and that surely the King never makes any mistakes, well, Gawain was the only logical culprit. *Quod erat demonstrandum.*

Flawless reasoning and logic somehow had the power to completely destroy the trust King Basil had had in Gawain, whom he also had loved as he would a son. And wasn't trust based on a relationship? And in this case, the relationship was between King Basil and Gawain, not Adrian.

Pixie meowed, concluding that this is why human beings get into so much trouble. Trust doesn't amount to much in their world, it seemed.

And maybe love doesn't either, thought the Philosopher, as she stroked her cat. King Basil had not only trusted Gawain but also loved him. And Gawain had trusted and loved King Basil too. This was just so horrible! How could this be?

The Philosopher read on. Gawain got dragged off to the castle dungeon. And there he sat on the cold floor, in shock of what had just happened. Why didn't King Basil trust him anymore? Why did he trust his Prime Minister more than he did Gawain? Did King Basil really trust the Prime Minister or just his apparently flawless logic? He was deeply hurt and felt King Basil had betrayed their bond, their deep trust and their love for each other.

The Philosopher imagined what Pixie must be thinking: Trust and love were the cornerstones of existence, yet flawless reasoning reigned in much of the western world and had the power somehow to erode such essential and deeply felt sentiments.

Reasoning by itself was a good thing, the Philosopher thought. That's what philosophers do — they reason things through.

But reasoning, the Philosopher reasoned, could be used for ill. That certainly seemed to be Adrian's intention — Adrian who, by the way, was quite envious of Gawain and the King's love for Gawain. Adrian had even discounted King Basil's feelings for Gawain as "irrational sentiments" when he made his case.

How could feelings as basic as trust and love be considered irrational, thought the Philosopher. That does not make any sense. And yet, more often than not, feelings were thought of as such for some reason. The Philosopher laughed at her use of the words *sense* and *reason* and how they can be used without any real thought.

Experts in the kingdom had now searched Gawain's house from top to bottom. They found nothing to corroborate the Prime Minister's accusation.

Yet the Prime Minister knew the stolen treasures must be somewhere and suggested Gawain be brought to trial. And King Basil agreed.

Can you imagine, Pixie? the Philosopher asked herself out loud. Can you just imagine? It seems as if *love* and *trust* are on trial, if you think about it. Love and trust had no real defense. Had they no place or voice in this?

Pixie jumped off the Philosopher's lap and made her way to the sofa bed in the room that was used as an office. Pixie lay down to take a nap.

The Philosopher continued reading the tale. Gawain was brought to trial and King Basil sat in the judge's seat. The Philosopher thought the whole plan might be flawed. Could a king be an impartial judge, especially when he doubted the defendant?

The whole town attended the trial, many of them Gawain's friends. Some had known him for a lifetime. Remember, the Philosopher reflected, that it's usually over time we learn that someone can be trusted. These friends who had known Gawain so long were now present at the trial. And they knew him to be a deeply honest and trustworthy goose.

All were appalled by the charges brought against Gawain. Gawain was not a thief. Never! Not Gawain! Justice would prevail.

But justice did not prevail, and the innocent was not declared innocent.

The townspeople had been persuaded and were now convinced that Gawain had deceived them all and that he had betrayed the trust they had in him, that he had now caused their distrust in him.

Interesting, thought the Philosopher, I'm sure Gawain felt that the townspeople were at fault for distrusting him, for he had done nothing wrong. He knew that much. This whole affair had now left him feeling betrayed by those he thought he could trust. Even his closest friends had all stopped believing in him.

Poor Gawain started doubting himself. Maybe he *had* done something wrong. But what? Maybe he *was* guilty, but of what?

The Philosopher set her book down on the side table next to her chair, stood up and walked over to her office to ask Pixie, How can reasoning have that kind of immediate effect? For one, no corroborating evidence was found, but that did not seem to matter, and for two, Gawain's character never came into the picture. All these years that he had been regarded as a truly honorable goose didn't seem to matter anymore, either. How could this be?

Pixie opened her eyes, yawned and gave the Philosopher what seemed like a dismissive look. The Philosopher read it to mean, You humans think that just because you have the biggest brains, you know everything. You may have the biggest brains, but you do not know how to *create* a world where love and trust reign.

In fact, the look continued to say, you use your big brains to destroy things. Look at the mess the world is in. What other than your big brains caused this destruction? Your brains got to your head, and in fact created the mess we are in now. Pixie was able to pack a lot of ideas into one look, the Philosopher thought.

Then Pixie closed her eyes, farted daintily and went back to sleep.

The Philosopher twitched her nose and decided that bigger brains truly did not guarantee anything. Like with any instrument — and the brain was an instrument of sorts — what mattered was how we used it.

But then again, the Philosopher wondered what, if not the brain, was in charge of *how* the brain was used?

The brain executes our ideas, but where are they originally formed? It was an intriguing question. The Philosopher decided it would be fun to think about some other time.

She returned to the couch and to her book and picked up where she left off. Pixie followed her and stretched out on the floor by her feet.

She turned to the page where King Basil ordered that Gawain be sent to the dungeon and stay there until he finally confessed where he had hidden the loot.

Gawain was enraged. No one had stood up for him. Why not? No one showed any compassion. Why not? They had all made up their minds somehow that *he* was the culprit — a thoroughly distrustful goose no one believed in anymore. And that was that. Why?

Why? Why? Why?

When the guards approached him to put him in irons and bring him down into the dungeon, Gawain saw a way out: The window was open! In no time, Gawain flew to freedom.

The crowd was aghast as they saw him fly high over the town and disappear into the forest further away.

The King too was outraged and vowed to track him down and bring him to justice.

Isn't it sad, the Philosopher thought, that two creatures who adored each other suddenly felt outraged by the other?

Pixie opened her eyes and stretched out her paws. The Philosopher watched her, wondering whether she was awake or asleep. Pixie must think that so much in our world had everything backwards. The innocent are guilty, and the guilty are innocent.

The Philosopher pondered the idea that we had a way of turning things upside down. Why did nobody stand up for Gawain? Why was his character so suddenly — in an instant — called into question? Why did even the King doubt him when he never had before?

Gawain had the keys to the Royal Treasury and that counted for everything, apparently. No one even tried to consider an alternative explanation for why some of the treasures had disappeared.

This troubled the Philosopher. If we say we value love and trust, then why are we so quick to give it up? What happened that we could so easily be convinced of the contrary?

Reclining Nude, 1948

Are we going against our better judgment and, if so, then why?

Ha! The Philosopher thought, where does this supposed better judgment come from? The same place our decisions come from? This was certainly something to contemplate.

The Philosopher looked down at Pixie, who was still lying at her feet and asked with a smile on her face, Would you fly out the window or allow yourself to be brought to the dungeon?

Pixie looked up at her as if to say, What a dumb question to ask!

Of course, the Philosopher said, you — being a cat — would take one bold leap and jump straight out the window. You would climb the tallest tree and wait until everyone had gone home. Then, at night, you would disappear into the darkness, never to be seen from again.

But oh, said the Philosopher, I'd be terribly sad if you did that, Pixie. I'd understand why you did it, but I would miss you so deeply. The Philosopher looked at her cat and wished that nothing would ever cause her to run away.

But what would I do? she asked herself. Would I fly away or stay? She laughed and thought about some of the philosophers she had read about and what they might do in the same circumstances.

Kant, for instance. Would Kant fly away?

No, she decided, he would probably stay. One of his written maxims stated that you could only act if you also willed it to be what he called universal law. So, if under universal law you felt that it was okay to fly out of the window and in that way escape the rule of law, there would be no point in having a rule of law. For this reason, Kant also concluded we should never lie, even to protect someone's life.

What good would universal law be if escaping the rule of law was not really an issue?

This may also explain why Socrates, the Philosopher thought, given the opportunity to flee Athens after he was unjustly accused of corrupting the youth, decided to respect the rule of law and drink the hemlock, which killed him.

Still Life, Paris, 1930

"...she could jump onto ... the highest shelf in the kitchen via the refrigerator."

Additionally, some might argue that you should stay, believing the truth would reveal itself in time. Why make it even *appear* as though you're guilty by flying away? Didn't flying out of the window make it look like you were escaping just punishment for what you had done, even if you hadn't done it?

Then she considered, What would Sartre do? For him, it would likely hinge on how you'd *decided for yourself.* Either way, it would not make that much difference in the end. Sartre believed in taking responsibility for your decisions, regardless of what they might be. Not universal law, but personal responsibility.

How about Nietzsche? Surely he would fly away. She laughed at the thought. Nietzsche was not going to subject himself to the utter stupidity of other people. Nietzsche himself was what he would call a master moralist. It occurred to the Philosopher that cats were the same: They own their own morality and are never dictated to by others. She smiled at the thought.

Nietzsche stressed the importance of living up to the responsibility of your own morality. Slave moralists, as he called them, only lived up to what others deemed moral.

So not only were you responsible for your own decisions, as Sartre would argue, you were in fact the master of your own destiny.

So, Pixie, like all other cats, may be very clear on what to do in such a situation. And she wouldn't be deterred by the jump itself. After all, she could jump onto the highest bookshelf via the adjacent cabinet or the highest shelf in the kitchen via the refrigerator. Pixie was an acrobat — she knew how to calculate her jumps with incredible accuracy and always landed quietly on her dainty paws. She, the Philosopher thought, would have no trouble jumping out the window! And she wouldn't hesitate for a second.

But human beings, on the other hand, could come up with so many opinions or rationalizations or whatevers on the matter. It was all rather confusing.

So, what would she do in Gawain's predicament? She looked at Pixie and decided she would dash out the window and follow her cat. She laughed, and Pixie seemed to grin at her as if to say, But of course!

Maybe, the Philosopher figured, continuing her train of thought, we tend to do what other people (or cats) do based on our *relationship* with them. She knew she trusted her cat and that meant that she would follow her compelling decision to leave the scene behind, plunging herself into the unknown, come what may. Now that's an example of trust if we ever saw one, she mused. Forget flawless reasoning; this was blind trust.

Maybe others, she continued, preferred to stay with what was familiar to them rather than fly off, desperately hoping that the truth would prevail sooner or later. But didn't Gawain also desperately hope the truth that he was indeed innocent would come out so he didn't have to live as a fugitive for the rest of his life?

And yet, whether languishing in the dungeon or fleeing and hiding as a fugitive on the run, either way, the truth may never come out. That too was a very real possibility.

Pixie journeyed over to the kitchen to snack on some of the cat food the Philosopher had put out for her, pleased that it was chicken, as she refused to eat anything else.

After her snack, she jumped on the Philosopher's lap and went to sleep. And just as the Philosopher trusted her cat, Pixie trusted her human — they were two beings that felt entirely comfortable and at home with each other.

The Philosopher continued reading the story. With Gawain gone, what happened next?

Right after Gawain departs, the story shifts to Derek the mouse.

At first, it's unclear what Derek has to do with anything. Derek was a friend of Gawain's, to be sure, but he mostly hung out with creatures more his own size.

He too had been present at the proceedings and had seen the whole event unfold. He noticed that no one had stood up for Gawain, not even him.

Pixie started to purr, perhaps expecting a possible turn of events or perhaps because she was simply a happy cat.

She shifted on the Philosopher's lap, always trying to find yet another more comfortable way to relax.

The thing is, Derek had found a small opening — remember, Derek was a mouse and was, thus, quite little — in the foot-thick wall of the Royal Treasury. He hadn't known where the opening led, but, being a mouse, of course, he had to find out what was on the other side of the wall.

And what did he see? King Basil had forgotten to turn down the lights in the Royal Treasury and Derek witnessed a glorious glow that looked like the northern lights. He couldn't believe his little eyes. This mysterious sight dazzled him.

Aha! The Philosopher mused, so King Basil — who never makes mistakes — *had* forgotten to turn down the lights. Let's remember that small but *significant* detail. She looked at Pixie with a glint in her eyes.

After some investigation, Derek discovered the source of the glow: a bright red ruby. It made the whole room glimmer. This got him thinking about his own humble abode. A bright red ruby that glowed like the northern lights would go a long way to cheering his rather drab-looking place up. And the King has so many, Derek thought, that even *if* he took this one, the King wouldn't even notice that he had taken it. And so, he took the dazzling gem.

Derek was right: After he added the bright red ruby, his home started to look so much more attractive. So, he went back and took a few more dark glowing rubies. Who would know?

Not only did his home take on a more commanding look, he felt *he* was becoming a mouse of consequence. He wanted to show off his rubies and share his joy with his cousin, but he decided that would be too risky. After all, these rubies were not really his.

And to whom did these treasures really belong? To King Basil, the Philosopher wondered, or to his kingdom and the subjects in his kingdom? That surely was something to consider as well.

She read on about what Derek did next. He gathered up some silver ornaments and brought them home too. Derek could not get enough of how enchanting his home started to look. He lit a few candles to enhance the effect of the glittering, glowing, sparkling treasures.

But in the process of creating this marvelous, magical world in his little home, Derek had also become greedy.

It was almost as if Pixie had seen it coming, yawning one big yawn. Why did so many of us always want more?

Sadly, Derek was no different.

He even imagined himself to be an emperor of his realm of creatures his size. He was someone now, but he was saddened by the fact that he could not share his rise in stature and immense pride and joy with anyone. In some ways, it made him feel lonelier, in fact. He would go out with an air of confidence, but then a sense of sadness would overtake him as well.

The Philosopher stroked her cat's back. This part of the story made her sad too.

Derek had meant no harm, but the situation didn't seem quite right either. He had stumbled upon the Royal Treasury by accident. If only King Basil had turned down the lights, the Philosopher thought. Who knows? Derek may not have been tempted by the warm glow of the red ruby. Not that this was any excuse, of course.

But she couldn't help thinking if the King had been less neglectful, things may not have turned out the way they did.

Anyway, Derek wasn't out to steal anything. And, really, all he wanted was to make his home more cheerful and beautiful. There was surely no harm in that.

People, too, she thought, wanted beautiful homes. But some were so eager to impress that they fell into the trap of always wanting more, never satisfied with what they had.

So, how did we become this way? The Philosopher asked herself. Why are we trying to be someone we are not? I mean, Derek was a happy mouse and was happy to be a mouse. But compared to the King with all his wealth, he suddenly felt he wanted something more, too, and something to brighten up his little, rather sad-looking home.

And why did the King live in such luxury and he, in contrast, in such lack of it? Was that even fair?

The Philosopher rolled her eyes up to the ceiling and thought that the issue of fairness was as basic as the issue of love and trust. We all had a sense of these things but were often led to believe that we could somehow manipulate and control them and turn them into what we needed at the time.

She decided to tackle this one some other time. But at the bottom of this rather complex notion of fairness was also the tendency we have of comparing ourselves to others, like the way Derek compared himself to the King. Derek now wanted to be a person of consequence, even though it had never crossed his mind before.

And where does that need come from? Does Pixie feel the need to compare herself to other cats? Or to dogs or other pets?

Pixie seemed to bristle at the thought. Pixie was Pixie and that was that.

"Pixie was Pixie and that was that."

She was someone not only in her own eyes, but also in the eyes of the Philosopher. I guess that made a real difference, the Philosopher thought. We want to be seen by others, but on what basis do we want to be seen? In a relationship, we feel seen. And can we really feel seen in this same way on the basis of wealth, or prestige or status?

It was clear to the Philosopher, however, that Pixie knew she was loved and seen by the Philosopher. That was the kind of wealth that mattered, she thought. And she and Pixie shared this wealth together.

The Philosopher enjoyed these side musings. And although she didn't quite purr like Pixie, she still felt quite pleased about the whole thing. After all, this was one of her favorite stories, precisely because it harbored so many questions we otherwise never ask ourselves — or do we? Do other people think about these things the way she did? The Philosopher wasn't quite sure. Or if they did, she wondered, why didn't they discuss these kinds of questions with each other more often?

Pixie yawned a big yawn, and the Philosopher turned her attention back to the story. She saw that the whole situation was now completely out of control.

Derek found the Kalikak diamond and brought that home too. But then he heard people talking about Gawain's upcoming trial. Everyone was talking about the scandal.

Derek felt utterly miserable. He was Gawain's friend and now look what he had done and how it had affected Gawain.

But instead of coming forward at the trial, Derek told himself that Gawain would probably be found innocent, which made Derek feel better. It would all turn out okay in the end.

But, as we already know, the Philosopher told Pixie, it didn't work out okay. Gawain was now going to be punished. The thought alone made Derek shiver.

Pixie had stirred at the Philosopher's voice. She decided to go think about things on her own, leaving the Philosopher's lap and heading towards the screen door of the balcony, which the Philosopher then opened for her. The Philosopher watched her jump up to her favorite spot on the balcony ledge where she could overlook her kingdom.

The Philosopher returned to her couch and turned back to the story, where Derek was in turmoil. How could a wise King make such an error of judgment, Derek considered. Likewise, could all his friends suddenly turn on him? What kind of friendship was that? And now that Gawain had been found guilty, why didn't he defend himself more?

Was Gawain a criminal? No! That was clear. But was he, Derek, a criminal? A crime had been committed, and he had committed the crime. So, was he a criminal? By all accounts, yes.

So, what actually made a criminal a criminal, the Philosopher wondered.

Would Pixie know?

The Philosopher decided to ask Pixie what made a criminal a criminal. She got up and visited Pixie on the balcony. Sure, the Philosopher said, seagulls and crows and all kinds of other animals "steal" things all the time from each other but were not thought of as criminals. She laughed, Only if you *own* something like jewels can the person who takes it from you be considered a criminal. By that definition, Derek was surely a criminal.

But did it also have to do with intent? she considered. Was it intent to do harm that made you a criminal? Derek didn't *intend* to do harm, but the harm done *was* substantial.

Following a train of thought, as always — and she had many running through her head — the Philosopher decided that maybe the Prime Minister was a *criminal by intent*. He took his jealousy out on Gawain and used his flawless reasoning to convince everyone of his guilt. And Derek was a criminal considering the harm he had caused.

The small mouse hadn't started out as a criminal, but did he somehow slip into being one? By justifying his actions that the King surely wouldn't miss a single ruby and that he only wanted to cheer up his little home, he figured he wasn't really doing anything wrong. Perhaps.

Meanwhile, Derek's reasoning had emboldened him to take more and more treasures back home. We are really good at rationalizing our actions, aren't we? the Philosopher thought.

With that, the Philosopher felt satisfied with Pixie's contributions to the whole affair and decided to leave her at peace to survey her territory.

The Philosopher continued to muse about Derek's intentions and actions, thinking this small mouse also did not know when or how to stop. Derek's own reasoning now had emboldened him to take more and more treasures back home. And he had now become a full-blown thief.

Maybe Derek didn't start off being greedy either, she thought, but slipped into it by always wanting more. Derek was surely guilty of that, stealing more and more from the treasury every day.

He also reasoned or rationalized that since Gawain was not guilty, he would be considered innocent — in other words, not guilty. However, that did not prove to be true at all. Until Derek showed that Gawain was in fact innocent, the whole community was going to see Gawain as a criminal who had deceived the King into believing that he could be trusted.

Derek was worried about Gawain too. Wherever he was, was he happy? Was he safe? He knew the King had sent out his guardsmen to track him down.

The Nun, 1929

Church in Veere, 1959

Consumed by misery, Derek started to reflect on what to do. He was going to prove Gawain's innocence by continuing to steal from the treasury at random — jewels, ornaments, money, whatever he could get his little mouse paws on.

That had the desired effect. Everyone in town was now convinced that Gawain was innocent. And all were shocked. They felt ashamed that they had allowed themselves to doubt Gawain's upright character. The King was devastated — how could he have doubted that Gawain had been speaking the truth when he said he was innocent?

The King had trusted Gawain, the Philosopher pondered, so why had he been so quick to distrust him when the rubies went missing? Why hadn't the King at least listened to Gawain with a fair and open mind? Did he feel that because he was so much more powerful than Gawain that he didn't have to listen to him? Maybe. And he was also very much convinced that he never made any mistakes — except, of course, for forgetting to turn down the lights in the Royal Treasury, the Philosopher mused with some sarcasm as she stood up to let Pixie in from the balcony.

She looked at Pixie and wondered how, if trust was so closely related to power, trust among humans must be quite different from that in the animal kingdom. Power did play a role in the animal world, of course, but wasn't competing with trust, or so it seemed. The King's willingness to distrust Gawain was perhaps related to his unbridled power, the Philosopher continued her thought, and now he deeply regretted his serious misjudgment.

The King had to find a way to make amends, so he sent out a whole troop to search for Gawain.

The Philosopher got up to prepare some salami on toast for lunch. Pixie leapt onto the countertop to watch her. The Philosopher scratched Pixie's chin and looked at her lovingly.

You're such an adorable cat, she said, and so intelligent. The Philosopher thought that Pixie seemed to truly understand *her* world in a way that humans rarely understand *their own*.

People were always trying to find answers to things, hoping to achieve a sense of certainty. Why not trust and embrace the world the way Pixie did? Pixie knew there was danger out in the world, but somehow it never undermined her sense of trust in the world. When she wandered outside, she was always vigilant and aware of the danger beyond her beloved Philosopher's apartment. There were different rules inside and outside the apartment, and she heeded both.

Danger and trust could exist side by side. But maybe trust and power could not? The Philosopher enjoyed thinking about her cat's view on the world. It helped put things into perspective and give her more confidence in finding a way to live her own life without always looking for certainty.

The Philosopher's mind returned to the story. Derek had proved Gawain's innocence, but more needed to be done. He didn't want to be seen as a thief in his own eyes, and so, slowly but surely, he started to carry the loot back to the Royal Treasury. That gave him a great sense of relief. Moreover, the King had called off the hunt to track Gawain down.

But Derek also thought that Gawain must be lonely and living with a feeling that everyone, including the King, thought of him as a criminal, a thief, a dishonorable goose who could never be trusted.

Again, the Philosopher asked herself, why were people so quick to misjudge others? Some people definitely deserved not to be trusted. That was true. Certainly, the Prime Minister should not have been trusted, no matter his clever reasoning that somehow convinced everyone.

But did misjudging others also seem to make one feel better or superior? Did it boost a false sense of self-esteem? Did we

The Chess Players, 1950

have to distrust and exclude others to feel more secure with those around us? All these thoughts ran through the Philosopher's head, and it made her dizzy.

Pixie, meanwhile, was at the door wanting to go out. Who could blame her, thought the Philosopher, as she opened the door for her. Pixie's outside world was not without danger, but it wasn't so full of misguided distrust — and misguided *trust*, too, she figured.

The Philosopher sat down and turned her attention back to the story, which explained what happened to Gawain after he fled out the window: He flew over the lake and into the woods. Thankfully, since then he was utterly exhausted, he found a concealed space under a rhododendron where he could rest. He quickly fell asleep.

The next morning, he moved about gingerly, knowing he was being hunted. He looked for breakfast, worms, tender shoots and bugs. He also realized he had to conceal his tracks, so he tied rushes to his yellow feet.

He looked down at his webbed feet and thought that at least his feet were real compared to everything else, which now seemed so strange and unreal to him.

Not knowing quite where to go or what to do, Gawain started to wander and soon found a cave at the edge of a cliff. He decided to make this cave his home. He made a barricade in front of the entrance so that you could barely look in. He finally felt safe.

He loved to go swimming in the lake but only felt comfortable doing so at night when the chances to be discovered were slim.

Gawain spent a lot of time recalling what happened that day. He remembered his friends, when they were still his friends and the warmth of the King's love for him. But what happened? If they had sincerely loved him, they would have believed him; so why didn't they?

The Guitar, 1930

The Philosopher had asked herself the same question and thought if they had all sincerely loved him, they would have at least given him the benefit of the doubt.

Where did the instant distrust come from? How did the Prime Minister's reasoning suddenly turn trust into distrust? Did it have to do with power once again — in this case, she wondered, the power of reasoning itself?

There was power in reasoning because it provided a sense of certainty, didn't it?

The Philosopher felt agitated. Something was wrong. She was deeply worried about something but wasn't sure what it was.

Then it struck her: Maybe some humans had put too much faith in reason alone, thinking they could solve things purely in their heads. But there was so much more to consider. The world — the universe, in fact — was infinite and how could all that fit into a finite box of logical reasoning?

The Philosopher let Pixie back inside. Although sometimes she wandered outside for hours, at other times she would go out for only a minute or two. Pixie had her own sense of time.

You really did have to think about things in their proper context, thought the Philosopher. If Gawain's insistence that he was innocent had been taken seriously based on how they all knew him, maybe they would have believed him and decided to continue the search for the real culprit.

Ah, she thought, maybe the need for certainty was driving the need to find someone to blame. They had found certainty at the expense of Gawain's innocence. That, alas, seems to be the case all too often.

Moreover, the King was believed to never make mistakes — even the King himself was convinced of that. The King, too, seemed to have a misguided sense of certainty simply based on the fact that he was King and therefore, in his view, *never makes mistakes.*

So, Adrian was able to manipulate this flaw in reasoning through convincing the crowd that surely it was Gawain who was to blame.

Ah! the Philosopher thought, was it our need for certainty that made us so quick to distrust something or someone?

Perhaps, because Pixie's world was less driven by a need to find certainty, it also did not need to find a false sense of certainty where there was none.

That was it; Adrian's reasoning about the keys had provided the townspeople with a misguided sense of certainty and made them heartless. What they knew about Gawain in their hearts was gone! Gawain had even been called *a disgrace to the kingdom*.

The Philosopher read on. This accusation of being a disgrace to the kingdom stuck in poor Gawain's brain and he often woke up in tears because of it. He simply could not understand how they had all abandoned him just like that.

After some time, he got somewhat used to his new life as a fugitive. He became a bit more relaxed and wandered off more, spending more time outside his cave and enjoying the daylight. He was careful but not scared. Vigilance had replaced fear.

Then one day, he came upon Derek the mouse and was elated. Finally, someone he could talk to. He had been so lonely with no one around.

They were both so surprised to see each other, until Gawain finally asked him what he was doing there.

Derek responded that he had been looking for Gawain. To which Gawain replied sarcastically, To bring me back to justice?

No, Derek assured him. They know it wasn't you. They called off the search party, knowing that you aren't guilty of the theft.

So, Gawain asked after a while, do they know who it was?

They don't, Derek answered, but I do. Derek admitted to Gawain he had stolen the treasures.

Gawain was still confused. If Derek hadn't told them he'd been the one stealing, how did they find out that it wasn't Gawain?

Song, 1959

Demonic Mirror, 1950

Well, Derek explained, because he had continued stealing to prove Gawain's innocence.

Derek told Gawain the whole story. At times Derek cried, feeling awful about how Gawain must have suffered. He cried with the relief of guilt and his secret that he'd been quiet about this whole time.

Gawain, too, cried, feeling relieved but also angry with his friends and the King who had all betrayed not just him but also their love for him.

Because that was what it was, wasn't it? the Philosopher thought. In the end, they had really betrayed their love for Gawain to the point that Gawain believed they could never have possibly loved him in the first place.

But they are suffering too, Derek told Gawain. They now feel horrible about how they have treated you.

Gawain could not feel sorry for his so-called friends or the King. He didn't care that they too had suffered. Let them suffer, he told Derek, adding that he never wanted to see them again, ever!

Derek touched Gawain's grooved leg, acknowledging that he understood, but also urging him to think again.

How powerful the touch of another being could be. Derek's gentle touch melted Gawain's heart and with it, his anger somehow evaporated.

Gawain succumbed to the soft touch of his friend and relented. Yes, he did want to see them again. He did!

Again, the Philosopher thought, the idea of power came up, but this time in such a positive way. This time it was the power to heal through touch — the touch of a common soul.

The Philosopher certainly did understand, knowing how a touch between Pixie and herself could be so soothing.

The power of Derek's touch reminded Gawain that we are deeply connected to each other and that he did want to live happily among his friends again, but now in a wiser way.

Pixie sauntered to the window to look out.

The Philosopher thought more about what had changed for Gawain. Seeing the world in a wiser way, she speculated, meant knowing that the world was not always fair and just and never would be but also acknowledging that we have a deep connection to this world and to each other at all times.

It wasn't until Derek had touched Gawain's leg that Gawain was reminded of how deeply connected he *did* feel to his friends and the King, even though they had betrayed him and their trust in him.

Gawain asked Derek whether he was going to confess, whereupon Derek responded that he would. He felt that he deserved to be punished.

A conversation about the nature of punishment ensued between the two friends and both Gawain and Derek finally decided that since everyone had suffered enough as it was, the idea of punishment seemed senseless at this point. Again, the Philosopher pondered how we should really think about matters such as these more thoroughly and discuss them with each other the way Gawain and Derek did.

If punishment was meant to make you suffer in order for you to mend your ways, well, Derek had already suffered plenty. And so had the King and all the townsfolk.

Justice had been served by the fact that everyone, including the King, had come to see their unjust treatment of Gawain. They were deeply humbled by admitting that they had done him wrong.

The Philosopher laughed at the idea that although we seem so driven by reason, we can end up being so unreasonable. On the other hand, it wasn't punishment alone that made us mend our ways; it was also our deep sense of connection to each other.

Pixie walked away from the window and threw her little body on the floor in front of the Philosopher, as though she approved of how this story was concluding.

In the end, Derek came up with the idea that they would walk back into town together and only the two of them would ever know what really happened. Now this seemed to be a very reasonable solution, truly!

Ha! thought the Philosopher, throwing an element of uncertainty as to who had stolen the King's jewels meant that this desire for certainty did have its limits, didn't it? There is no such thing as absolute certainty.

The story had a happy ending — knowing that happiness does not depend on absolute certainty. Without any knowledge of who had in fact stolen from the Royal Treasury, the townsfolk welcomed them back and once again showed their love and admiration for Gawain. And to show his appreciation for him, the King made Gawain the Royal Architect.

Gawain had always dreamed of being a great architect. And now he was given the task of designing a new opera house. He decided it ought to be in the form of an egg and that Derek was just the mouse to help him with the job. Derek would act as the Royal Architect's assistant.

After the Philosopher finished the story, she let Pixie go back outside. The Philosopher was left with so much more to ponder about the power of uncertainty. Then she laughed, thinking how that was perfect because philosophers are experts in not-knowing. And that we should be happy about this state of uncertainty since not-knowing makes the world better.

Nature morte avec citron, 1924

She looked out of her big living room window and gazed at her philosopher's cat, who had found a comfortable place to lie down in the grass in the sun. Pixie's sheer presence in her life always provided the Philosopher with so much more to think about.

Then the Philosopher sat on her couch and looked at one of her grandfather's paintings. She got lost in it. Although it was unfinished, she loved his use of colors. She thought about how he'd developed his own color theory and put it to use in all his artwork. Somehow, not unlike Pixie, her grandfather had always given her another way of looking at the world. She could even see herself in this painting — she, a philosopher, and her cat. His artwork also revealed a sense of reality that deeply influenced her understanding of the world. The world with its many facets, like windows through which to see from all different angles. And although not one window revealed the full picture or provided true certainty about the world outside, each offered a perspective and added to a rich, nuanced and meaningful life.

The Philosopher and her cat.

www.ingramcontent.com/pod-product-compliance
Lightning Source LLC
LaVergne TN
LVHW010305070426
835507LV00027B/3448